THIS SWIMMING JOURNAL BELONGS TO

_____

_____

*"Swimmers don't quit.
Quitters don't swim."*

TABLE OF CONTENTS

Training Log 1

Personal Records 101

Notes 117

TRAINING LOG

Date: _____ Time: _____

Warm Up

Swim Activity	Distance	Reps	Time	Rest

Sets

Swim Activity	Distance	Reps	Time	Rest

Cool Down

Swim Activity	Distance	Reps	Time	Rest

Difficulty: 🏊 🏊 🏊   Rating: ★ ★ ★ ★ ★

TRAINING LOG

Date: _____ Time: _____

Warm Up

Swim Activity	Distance	Reps	Time	Rest

Sets

Swim Activity	Distance	Reps	Time	Rest

Cool Down

Swim Activity	Distance	Reps	Time	Rest

Difficulty: 🏊 🏊 🏊   Rating: ★ ★ ★ ★ ★

TRAINING LOG

Date: _____ Time: _____

Warm Up

Swim Activity	Distance	Reps	Time	Rest

Sets

Swim Activity	Distance	Reps	Time	Rest

Cool Down

Swim Activity	Distance	Reps	Time	Rest

Difficulty: 🏊 🏊 🏊   Rating: ★ ★ ★ ★ ★

TRAINING LOG

Date: _____ Time: _____

Warm Up

Swim Activity	Distance	Reps	Time	Rest

Sets

Swim Activity	Distance	Reps	Time	Rest

Cool Down

Swim Activity	Distance	Reps	Time	Rest

Difficulty: Rating:

── TRAINING LOG ──

Date: _____ Time: _____

Warm Up

Swim Activity	Distance	Reps	Time	Rest

Sets

Swim Activity	Distance	Reps	Time	Rest

Cool Down

Swim Activity	Distance	Reps	Time	Rest

Difficulty: 🏊 🏊 🏊   Rating: ★ ★ ★ ★ ★

TRAINING LOG

Date: _____ Time: _____

Warm Up

Swim Activity	Distance	Reps	Time	Rest

Sets

Swim Activity	Distance	Reps	Time	Rest

Cool Down

Swim Activity	Distance	Reps	Time	Rest

Difficulty: Rating:

TRAINING LOG

Date: _____ Time: _____

Warm Up

Swim Activity	Distance	Reps	Time	Rest

Sets

Swim Activity	Distance	Reps	Time	Rest

Cool Down

Swim Activity	Distance	Reps	Time	Rest

Difficulty: 🏊 🏊 🏊   Rating: ★ ★ ★ ★ ★

TRAINING LOG

Date: _____ Time: _____

Warm Up

Swim Activity	Distance	Reps	Time	Rest

Sets

Swim Activity	Distance	Reps	Time	Rest

Cool Down

Swim Activity	Distance	Reps	Time	Rest

Difficulty: Rating:

TRAINING LOG

Date: _____ Time: _____

Warm Up

Swim Activity	Distance	Reps	Time	Rest

Sets

Swim Activity	Distance	Reps	Time	Rest

Cool Down

Swim Activity	Distance	Reps	Time	Rest

Difficulty: Rating:

TRAINING LOG

Date: _____ Time: _____

Warm Up

Swim Activity	Distance	Reps	Time	Rest

Sets

Swim Activity	Distance	Reps	Time	Rest

Cool Down

Swim Activity	Distance	Reps	Time	Rest

Difficulty: 🏊 🏊 🏊   Rating: ★ ★ ★ ★ ★

━━ TRAINING LOG ━━

Date: _____ Time: _____

Warm Up

Swim Activity	Distance	Reps	Time	Rest

Sets

Swim Activity	Distance	Reps	Time	Rest

Cool Down

Swim Activity	Distance	Reps	Time	Rest

Difficulty: 🏊 🏊 🏊   Rating: ★ ★ ★ ★ ★

TRAINING LOG

Date: _____ Time: _____

Warm Up

Swim Activity	Distance	Reps	Time	Rest

Sets

Swim Activity	Distance	Reps	Time	Rest

Cool Down

Swim Activity	Distance	Reps	Time	Rest

Difficulty: Rating:

TRAINING LOG

Date: _____ Time: _____

Warm Up

Swim Activity	Distance	Reps	Time	Rest

Sets

Swim Activity	Distance	Reps	Time	Rest

Cool Down

Swim Activity	Distance	Reps	Time	Rest

Difficulty: 🏊 🏊 🏊   Rating: ★ ★ ★ ★ ★

TRAINING LOG

Date: _____ Time: _____

Warm Up

Swim Activity	Distance	Reps	Time	Rest

Sets

Swim Activity	Distance	Reps	Time	Rest

Cool Down

Swim Activity	Distance	Reps	Time	Rest

Difficulty: Rating:

── TRAINING LOG ──

Date: _____ Time: _____

Warm Up

Swim Activity	Distance	Reps	Time	Rest

Sets

Swim Activity	Distance	Reps	Time	Rest

Cool Down

Swim Activity	Distance	Reps	Time	Rest

Difficulty: 🏊 🏊 🏊   Rating: ★ ★ ★ ★ ★

TRAINING LOG

Date: _____ Time: _____

Warm Up

Swim Activity	Distance	Reps	Time	Rest

Sets

Swim Activity	Distance	Reps	Time	Rest

Cool Down

Swim Activity	Distance	Reps	Time	Rest

Difficulty: 🏊 🏊 🏊   Rating: ★ ★ ★ ★ ★

TRAINING LOG

Date: _____ Time: _____

Warm Up

Swim Activity	Distance	Reps	Time	Rest

Sets

Swim Activity	Distance	Reps	Time	Rest

Cool Down

Swim Activity	Distance	Reps	Time	Rest

Difficulty: 🏊 🏊 🏊   Rating: ★ ★ ★ ★ ★

TRAINING LOG

Date: _____ Time: _____

Warm Up

Swim Activity	Distance	Reps	Time	Rest

Sets

Swim Activity	Distance	Reps	Time	Rest

Cool Down

Swim Activity	Distance	Reps	Time	Rest

Difficulty: Rating:

— TRAINING LOG —

Date: _____ Time: _____

Warm Up

Swim Activity	Distance	Reps	Time	Rest

Sets

Swim Activity	Distance	Reps	Time	Rest

Cool Down

Swim Activity	Distance	Reps	Time	Rest

Difficulty: 🏊 🏊 🏊   Rating: ★ ★ ★ ★ ★

TRAINING LOG

Date: _____ Time: _____

Warm Up

Swim Activity	Distance	Reps	Time	Rest

Sets

Swim Activity	Distance	Reps	Time	Rest

Cool Down

Swim Activity	Distance	Reps	Time	Rest

Difficulty: Rating:

TRAINING LOG

Date: _____ Time: _____

Warm Up

Swim Activity	Distance	Reps	Time	Rest

Sets

Swim Activity	Distance	Reps	Time	Rest

Cool Down

Swim Activity	Distance	Reps	Time	Rest

Difficulty: 🏊 🏊 🏊   Rating: ★ ★ ★ ★ ★

TRAINING LOG

Date: _____ Time: _____

Warm Up

Swim Activity	Distance	Reps	Time	Rest

Sets

Swim Activity	Distance	Reps	Time	Rest

Cool Down

Swim Activity	Distance	Reps	Time	Rest

Difficulty: 🏊 🏊 🏊   Rating: ★ ★ ★ ★ ★

── TRAINING LOG ──

Date: _____ Time: _____

Warm Up

Swim Activity	Distance	Reps	Time	Rest

Sets

Swim Activity	Distance	Reps	Time	Rest

Cool Down

Swim Activity	Distance	Reps	Time	Rest

Difficulty: 🏊 🏊 🏊   Rating: ★ ★ ★ ★ ★

TRAINING LOG

Date: _____ Time: _____

Warm Up

Swim Activity	Distance	Reps	Time	Rest

Sets

Swim Activity	Distance	Reps	Time	Rest

Cool Down

Swim Activity	Distance	Reps	Time	Rest

Difficulty: Rating:

——— TRAINING LOG ———

Date: _____ Time: _____

Warm Up				
Swim Activity	Distance	Reps	Time	Rest

Sets				
Swim Activity	Distance	Reps	Time	Rest

Cool Down				
Swim Activity	Distance	Reps	Time	Rest

Difficulty: 🏊 🏊 🏊   Rating: ★ ★ ★ ★ ★

TRAINING LOG

Date: _____ Time: _____

Warm Up

Swim Activity	Distance	Reps	Time	Rest

Sets

Swim Activity	Distance	Reps	Time	Rest

Cool Down

Swim Activity	Distance	Reps	Time	Rest

Difficulty: Rating:

TRAINING LOG

Date: _____ Time: _____

Warm Up

Swim Activity	Distance	Reps	Time	Rest

Sets

Swim Activity	Distance	Reps	Time	Rest

Cool Down

Swim Activity	Distance	Reps	Time	Rest

Difficulty: Rating:

TRAINING LOG

Date: _____ Time: _____

Warm Up

Swim Activity	Distance	Reps	Time	Rest

Sets

Swim Activity	Distance	Reps	Time	Rest

Cool Down

Swim Activity	Distance	Reps	Time	Rest

Difficulty: Rating:

TRAINING LOG

Date: _____ Time: _____

Warm Up

Swim Activity	Distance	Reps	Time	Rest

Sets

Swim Activity	Distance	Reps	Time	Rest

Cool Down

Swim Activity	Distance	Reps	Time	Rest

Difficulty: 🏊 🏊 🏊   Rating: ★ ★ ★ ★ ★

TRAINING LOG

Date: _____ Time: _____

Warm Up

Swim Activity	Distance	Reps	Time	Rest

Sets

Swim Activity	Distance	Reps	Time	Rest

Cool Down

Swim Activity	Distance	Reps	Time	Rest

Difficulty: Rating:

TRAINING LOG

Date: _____ Time: _____

Warm Up

Swim Activity	Distance	Reps	Time	Rest

Sets

Swim Activity	Distance	Reps	Time	Rest

Cool Down

Swim Activity	Distance	Reps	Time	Rest

Difficulty: 🏊 🏊 🏊   Rating: ★ ★ ★ ★ ★

TRAINING LOG

Date: _____ Time: _____

Warm Up

Swim Activity	Distance	Reps	Time	Rest

Sets

Swim Activity	Distance	Reps	Time	Rest

Cool Down

Swim Activity	Distance	Reps	Time	Rest

Difficulty: Rating:

TRAINING LOG

Date: _____ Time: _____

Warm Up

Swim Activity	Distance	Reps	Time	Rest

Sets

Swim Activity	Distance	Reps	Time	Rest

Cool Down

Swim Activity	Distance	Reps	Time	Rest

Difficulty: Rating: ★ ★ ★ ★ ★

TRAINING LOG

Date: _____ Time: _____

Warm Up

Swim Activity	Distance	Reps	Time	Rest

Sets

Swim Activity	Distance	Reps	Time	Rest

Cool Down

Swim Activity	Distance	Reps	Time	Rest

Difficulty: 🏊 🏊 🏊   Rating: ★ ★ ★ ★ ★

TRAINING LOG

Date: _____ Time: _____

Warm Up

Swim Activity	Distance	Reps	Time	Rest

Sets

Swim Activity	Distance	Reps	Time	Rest

Cool Down

Swim Activity	Distance	Reps	Time	Rest

Difficulty: 🏊 🏊 🏊   Rating: ★ ★ ★ ★ ★

TRAINING LOG

Date: _____ Time: _____

Warm Up

Swim Activity	Distance	Reps	Time	Rest

Sets

Swim Activity	Distance	Reps	Time	Rest

Cool Down

Swim Activity	Distance	Reps	Time	Rest

Difficulty: 🏊 🏊 🏊   Rating: ★ ★ ★ ★ ★

TRAINING LOG

Date: _____ Time: _____

Warm Up

Swim Activity	Distance	Reps	Time	Rest

Sets

Swim Activity	Distance	Reps	Time	Rest

Cool Down

Swim Activity	Distance	Reps	Time	Rest

Difficulty: 🏊 🏊 🏊   Rating: ★ ★ ★ ★ ★

TRAINING LOG

Date: _____ Time: _____

Warm Up

Swim Activity	Distance	Reps	Time	Rest

Sets

Swim Activity	Distance	Reps	Time	Rest

Cool Down

Swim Activity	Distance	Reps	Time	Rest

Difficulty: Rating:

TRAINING LOG

Date: _____ Time: _____

Warm Up

Swim Activity	Distance	Reps	Time	Rest

Sets

Swim Activity	Distance	Reps	Time	Rest

Cool Down

Swim Activity	Distance	Reps	Time	Rest

Difficulty: 🏊 🏊 🏊 Rating: ★ ★ ★ ★ ★

TRAINING LOG

Date: _____ Time: _____

Warm Up

Swim Activity	Distance	Reps	Time	Rest

Sets

Swim Activity	Distance	Reps	Time	Rest

Cool Down

Swim Activity	Distance	Reps	Time	Rest

Difficulty: Rating:

TRAINING LOG

Date: _____ Time: _____

Warm Up

Swim Activity	Distance	Reps	Time	Rest

Sets

Swim Activity	Distance	Reps	Time	Rest

Cool Down

Swim Activity	Distance	Reps	Time	Rest

Difficulty: 🏊 🏊 🏊   Rating: ★ ★ ★ ★ ★

TRAINING LOG

Date: _____ Time: _____

Warm Up

Swim Activity	Distance	Reps	Time	Rest

Sets

Swim Activity	Distance	Reps	Time	Rest

Cool Down

Swim Activity	Distance	Reps	Time	Rest

Difficulty: Rating:

TRAINING LOG

Date: _____ Time: _____

Warm Up

Swim Activity	Distance	Reps	Time	Rest

Sets

Swim Activity	Distance	Reps	Time	Rest

Cool Down

Swim Activity	Distance	Reps	Time	Rest

Difficulty: Rating:

TRAINING LOG

Date: _____ Time: _____

Warm Up

Swim Activity	Distance	Reps	Time	Rest

Sets

Swim Activity	Distance	Reps	Time	Rest

Cool Down

Swim Activity	Distance	Reps	Time	Rest

Difficulty: Rating:

TRAINING LOG

Date: _____ Time: _____

Warm Up

Swim Activity	Distance	Reps	Time	Rest

Sets

Swim Activity	Distance	Reps	Time	Rest

Cool Down

Swim Activity	Distance	Reps	Time	Rest

Difficulty: 🏊 🏊 🏊   Rating: ★ ★ ★ ★ ★

TRAINING LOG

Date: _____ Time: _____

Warm Up

Swim Activity	Distance	Reps	Time	Rest

Sets

Swim Activity	Distance	Reps	Time	Rest

Cool Down

Swim Activity	Distance	Reps	Time	Rest

Difficulty: Rating:

── TRAINING LOG ──

Date: _____ Time: _____

Warm Up

Swim Activity	Distance	Reps	Time	Rest

Sets

Swim Activity	Distance	Reps	Time	Rest

Cool Down

Swim Activity	Distance	Reps	Time	Rest

Difficulty: 🏊 🏊 🏊   Rating: ★ ★ ★ ★ ★

TRAINING LOG

Date: _____ Time: _____

Warm Up

Swim Activity	Distance	Reps	Time	Rest

Sets

Swim Activity	Distance	Reps	Time	Rest

Cool Down

Swim Activity	Distance	Reps	Time	Rest

Difficulty: 🏊 🏊 🏊   Rating: ★ ★ ★ ★ ★

TRAINING LOG

Date: _____ Time: _____

Warm Up

Swim Activity	Distance	Reps	Time	Rest

Sets

Swim Activity	Distance	Reps	Time	Rest

Cool Down

Swim Activity	Distance	Reps	Time	Rest

Difficulty:　　　　　　　　　　Rating:

TRAINING LOG

Date: _____ Time: _____

Warm Up

Swim Activity	Distance	Reps	Time	Rest

Sets

Swim Activity	Distance	Reps	Time	Rest

Cool Down

Swim Activity	Distance	Reps	Time	Rest

Difficulty: 🏊 🏊 🏊   Rating: ★ ★ ★ ★ ★

TRAINING LOG

Date: _____ Time: _____

Warm Up

Swim Activity	Distance	Reps	Time	Rest

Sets

Swim Activity	Distance	Reps	Time	Rest

Cool Down

Swim Activity	Distance	Reps	Time	Rest

Difficulty: 🏊 🏊 🏊   Rating: ★ ★ ★ ★ ★

TRAINING LOG

Date: _____ Time: _____

Warm Up

Swim Activity	Distance	Reps	Time	Rest

Sets

Swim Activity	Distance	Reps	Time	Rest

Cool Down

Swim Activity	Distance	Reps	Time	Rest

Difficulty: 🏊 🏊 🏊   Rating: ★ ★ ★ ★ ★

— TRAINING LOG —

Date: _____ Time: _____

Warm Up

Swim Activity	Distance	Reps	Time	Rest

Sets

Swim Activity	Distance	Reps	Time	Rest

Cool Down

Swim Activity	Distance	Reps	Time	Rest

Difficulty: 🏊 🏊 🏊   Rating: ★ ★ ★ ★ ★

── TRAINING LOG ──

Date: _____ Time: _____

Warm Up

Swim Activity	Distance	Reps	Time	Rest

Sets

Swim Activity	Distance	Reps	Time	Rest

Cool Down

Swim Activity	Distance	Reps	Time	Rest

Difficulty: 🏊 🏊 🏊   Rating: ★ ★ ★ ★ ★

TRAINING LOG

Date: _____ Time: _____

Warm Up

Swim Activity	Distance	Reps	Time	Rest

Sets

Swim Activity	Distance	Reps	Time	Rest

Cool Down

Swim Activity	Distance	Reps	Time	Rest

Difficulty:　　　　　　　　Rating:

TRAINING LOG

Date: _____ Time: _____

Warm Up

Swim Activity	Distance	Reps	Time	Rest

Sets

Swim Activity	Distance	Reps	Time	Rest

Cool Down

Swim Activity	Distance	Reps	Time	Rest

Difficulty: Rating:

TRAINING LOG

Date: _____ Time: _____

Warm Up

Swim Activity	Distance	Reps	Time	Rest

Sets

Swim Activity	Distance	Reps	Time	Rest

Cool Down

Swim Activity	Distance	Reps	Time	Rest

Difficulty: 🏊 🏊 🏊   Rating: ★ ★ ★ ★ ★

TRAINING LOG

Date: _____ Time: _____

Warm Up

Swim Activity	Distance	Reps	Time	Rest

Sets

Swim Activity	Distance	Reps	Time	Rest

Cool Down

Swim Activity	Distance	Reps	Time	Rest

Difficulty: 🏊 🏊 🏊   Rating: ★ ★ ★ ★ ★

TRAINING LOG

Date: _____ Time: _____

Warm Up

Swim Activity	Distance	Reps	Time	Rest

Sets

Swim Activity	Distance	Reps	Time	Rest

Cool Down

Swim Activity	Distance	Reps	Time	Rest

Difficulty: 🏊 🏊 🏊   Rating: ★ ★ ★ ★ ★

TRAINING LOG

Date: _____ Time: _____

Warm Up

Swim Activity	Distance	Reps	Time	Rest

Sets

Swim Activity	Distance	Reps	Time	Rest

Cool Down

Swim Activity	Distance	Reps	Time	Rest

Difficulty: Rating:

TRAINING LOG

Date: _____ Time: _____

Warm Up

Swim Activity	Distance	Reps	Time	Rest

Sets

Swim Activity	Distance	Reps	Time	Rest

Cool Down

Swim Activity	Distance	Reps	Time	Rest

Difficulty: Rating:

TRAINING LOG

Date: _____ Time: _____

Warm Up

Swim Activity	Distance	Reps	Time	Rest

Sets

Swim Activity	Distance	Reps	Time	Rest

Cool Down

Swim Activity	Distance	Reps	Time	Rest

Difficulty: 🏊 🏊 🏊   Rating: ★ ★ ★ ★ ★

TRAINING LOG

Date: _____ Time: _____

Warm Up

Swim Activity	Distance	Reps	Time	Rest

Sets

Swim Activity	Distance	Reps	Time	Rest

Cool Down

Swim Activity	Distance	Reps	Time	Rest

Difficulty: 🏊 🏊 🏊   Rating: ★ ★ ★ ★ ★

TRAINING LOG

Date: _____ Time: _____

Warm Up

Swim Activity	Distance	Reps	Time	Rest

Sets

Swim Activity	Distance	Reps	Time	Rest

Cool Down

Swim Activity	Distance	Reps	Time	Rest

Difficulty: 🏊 🏊 🏊   Rating: ★ ★ ★ ★ ★

TRAINING LOG

Date: _____ Time: _____

Warm Up

Swim Activity	Distance	Reps	Time	Rest

Sets

Swim Activity	Distance	Reps	Time	Rest

Cool Down

Swim Activity	Distance	Reps	Time	Rest

Difficulty: 🏊 🏊 🏊   Rating: ★ ★ ★ ★ ★

TRAINING LOG

Date: _____ Time: _____

Warm Up

Swim Activity	Distance	Reps	Time	Rest

Sets

Swim Activity	Distance	Reps	Time	Rest

Cool Down

Swim Activity	Distance	Reps	Time	Rest

Difficulty: 🏊 🏊 🏊   Rating: ★ ★ ★ ★ ★

TRAINING LOG

Date: _____ Time: _____

Warm Up

Swim Activity	Distance	Reps	Time	Rest

Sets

Swim Activity	Distance	Reps	Time	Rest

Cool Down

Swim Activity	Distance	Reps	Time	Rest

Difficulty: 🏊 🏊 🏊   Rating: ★ ★ ★ ★ ★

TRAINING LOG

Date: _____ Time: _____

Warm Up

Swim Activity	Distance	Reps	Time	Rest

Sets

Swim Activity	Distance	Reps	Time	Rest

Cool Down

Swim Activity	Distance	Reps	Time	Rest

Difficulty: Rating:

TRAINING LOG

Date: _____ Time: _____

Warm Up

Swim Activity	Distance	Reps	Time	Rest

Sets

Swim Activity	Distance	Reps	Time	Rest

Cool Down

Swim Activity	Distance	Reps	Time	Rest

Difficulty: 🏊 🏊 🏊   Rating: ★ ★ ★ ★ ★

TRAINING LOG

Date: _____ Time: _____

Warm Up

Swim Activity	Distance	Reps	Time	Rest

Sets

Swim Activity	Distance	Reps	Time	Rest

Cool Down

Swim Activity	Distance	Reps	Time	Rest

Difficulty: 🏊 🏊 🏊   Rating: ⭐ ⭐ ⭐ ⭐ ⭐

TRAINING LOG

Date: _____ Time: _____

Warm Up

Swim Activity	Distance	Reps	Time	Rest

Sets

Swim Activity	Distance	Reps	Time	Rest

Cool Down

Swim Activity	Distance	Reps	Time	Rest

Difficulty: 🏊 🏊 🏊   Rating: ★ ★ ★ ★ ★

TRAINING LOG

Date: _____ Time: _____

Warm Up

Swim Activity	Distance	Reps	Time	Rest

Sets

Swim Activity	Distance	Reps	Time	Rest

Cool Down

Swim Activity	Distance	Reps	Time	Rest

Difficulty: Rating:

TRAINING LOG

Date: _____ Time: _____

Warm Up

Swim Activity	Distance	Reps	Time	Rest

Sets

Swim Activity	Distance	Reps	Time	Rest

Cool Down

Swim Activity	Distance	Reps	Time	Rest

Difficulty: 🏊 🏊 🏊   Rating: ★ ★ ★ ★ ★

TRAINING LOG

Date: _____ Time: _____

Warm Up

Swim Activity	Distance	Reps	Time	Rest

Sets

Swim Activity	Distance	Reps	Time	Rest

Cool Down

Swim Activity	Distance	Reps	Time	Rest

Difficulty: 🏊 🏊 🏊   Rating: ★ ★ ★ ★ ★

TRAINING LOG

Date: _____ Time: _____

Warm Up

Swim Activity	Distance	Reps	Time	Rest

Sets

Swim Activity	Distance	Reps	Time	Rest

Cool Down

Swim Activity	Distance	Reps	Time	Rest

Difficulty: Rating:

TRAINING LOG

Date: _____ Time: _____

Warm Up

Swim Activity	Distance	Reps	Time	Rest

Sets

Swim Activity	Distance	Reps	Time	Rest

Cool Down

Swim Activity	Distance	Reps	Time	Rest

Difficulty: Rating:

TRAINING LOG

Date: _____ Time: _____

Warm Up

Swim Activity	Distance	Reps	Time	Rest

Sets

Swim Activity	Distance	Reps	Time	Rest

Cool Down

Swim Activity	Distance	Reps	Time	Rest

Difficulty: 🏊 🏊 🏊 Rating: ★ ★ ★ ★ ★

TRAINING LOG

Date: _____ Time: _____

Warm Up

Swim Activity	Distance	Reps	Time	Rest

Sets

Swim Activity	Distance	Reps	Time	Rest

Cool Down

Swim Activity	Distance	Reps	Time	Rest

Difficulty: 🏊 🏊 🏊   Rating: ★ ★ ★ ★ ★

TRAINING LOG

Date: _____ Time: _____

Warm Up

Swim Activity	Distance	Reps	Time	Rest

Sets

Swim Activity	Distance	Reps	Time	Rest

Cool Down

Swim Activity	Distance	Reps	Time	Rest

Difficulty: 🏊 🏊 🏊   Rating: ★ ★ ★ ★ ★

TRAINING LOG

Date: _____ Time: _____

Warm Up

Swim Activity	Distance	Reps	Time	Rest

Sets

Swim Activity	Distance	Reps	Time	Rest

Cool Down

Swim Activity	Distance	Reps	Time	Rest

Difficulty: 　　　　　　Rating:

TRAINING LOG

Date: _____ Time: _____

Warm Up

Swim Activity	Distance	Reps	Time	Rest

Sets

Swim Activity	Distance	Reps	Time	Rest

Cool Down

Swim Activity	Distance	Reps	Time	Rest

Difficulty: 🏊 🏊 🏊   Rating: ★ ★ ★ ★ ★

TRAINING LOG

Date: _____ Time: _____

Warm Up

Swim Activity	Distance	Reps	Time	Rest

Sets

Swim Activity	Distance	Reps	Time	Rest

Cool Down

Swim Activity	Distance	Reps	Time	Rest

Difficulty: Rating:

TRAINING LOG

Date: _____ Time: _____

Warm Up

Swim Activity	Distance	Reps	Time	Rest

Sets

Swim Activity	Distance	Reps	Time	Rest

Cool Down

Swim Activity	Distance	Reps	Time	Rest

Difficulty: 🏊 🏊 🏊   Rating: ★ ★ ★ ★ ★

TRAINING LOG

Date: _____ Time: _____

Warm Up

Swim Activity	Distance	Reps	Time	Rest

Sets

Swim Activity	Distance	Reps	Time	Rest

Cool Down

Swim Activity	Distance	Reps	Time	Rest

Difficulty: 🏊 🏊 🏊   Rating: ★ ★ ★ ★ ★

TRAINING LOG

Date: _____ Time: _____

Warm Up

Swim Activity	Distance	Reps	Time	Rest

Sets

Swim Activity	Distance	Reps	Time	Rest

Cool Down

Swim Activity	Distance	Reps	Time	Rest

Difficulty: 🏊 🏊 🏊   Rating: ★ ★ ★ ★ ★

TRAINING LOG

Date: _____ Time: _____

Warm Up

Swim Activity	Distance	Reps	Time	Rest

Sets

Swim Activity	Distance	Reps	Time	Rest

Cool Down

Swim Activity	Distance	Reps	Time	Rest

Difficulty: 🏊 🏊 🏊   Rating: ★ ★ ★ ★ ★

TRAINING LOG

Date: _____ Time: _____

Warm Up

Swim Activity	Distance	Reps	Time	Rest

Sets

Swim Activity	Distance	Reps	Time	Rest

Cool Down

Swim Activity	Distance	Reps	Time	Rest

Difficulty: Rating:

TRAINING LOG

Date: _____ Time: _____

Warm Up

Swim Activity	Distance	Reps	Time	Rest

Sets

Swim Activity	Distance	Reps	Time	Rest

Cool Down

Swim Activity	Distance	Reps	Time	Rest

Difficulty: Rating:

── **TRAINING LOG** ──

Date: _____ Time: _____

Warm Up

Swim Activity	Distance	Reps	Time	Rest

Sets

Swim Activity	Distance	Reps	Time	Rest

Cool Down

Swim Activity	Distance	Reps	Time	Rest

Difficulty: 🏊 🏊 🏊   Rating: ★ ★ ★ ★ ★

TRAINING LOG

Date: _____ Time: _____

Warm Up

Swim Activity	Distance	Reps	Time	Rest

Sets

Swim Activity	Distance	Reps	Time	Rest

Cool Down

Swim Activity	Distance	Reps	Time	Rest

Difficulty: Rating:

TRAINING LOG

Date: _____ Time: _____

Warm Up

Swim Activity	Distance	Reps	Time	Rest

Sets

Swim Activity	Distance	Reps	Time	Rest

Cool Down

Swim Activity	Distance	Reps	Time	Rest

Difficulty: Rating:

TRAINING LOG

Date: _____ Time: _____

Warm Up

Swim Activity	Distance	Reps	Time	Rest

Sets

Swim Activity	Distance	Reps	Time	Rest

Cool Down

Swim Activity	Distance	Reps	Time	Rest

Difficulty: 🏊 🏊 🏊   Rating: ⭐ ⭐ ⭐ ⭐ ⭐

TRAINING LOG

Date: _____   Time: _____

Warm Up

Swim Activity	Distance	Reps	Time	Rest

Sets

Swim Activity	Distance	Reps	Time	Rest

Cool Down

Swim Activity	Distance	Reps	Time	Rest

Difficulty: Rating:

TRAINING LOG

Date: _____ Time: _____

Warm Up

Swim Activity	Distance	Reps	Time	Rest

Sets

Swim Activity	Distance	Reps	Time	Rest

Cool Down

Swim Activity	Distance	Reps	Time	Rest

Difficulty: Rating:

TRAINING LOG

Date: _____ Time: _____

Warm Up

Swim Activity	Distance	Reps	Time	Rest

Sets

Swim Activity	Distance	Reps	Time	Rest

Cool Down

Swim Activity	Distance	Reps	Time	Rest

Difficulty: 🏊 🏊 🏊   Rating: ★ ★ ★ ★ ★

TRAINING LOG

Date: _____ Time: _____

Warm Up

Swim Activity	Distance	Reps	Time	Rest

Sets

Swim Activity	Distance	Reps	Time	Rest

Cool Down

Swim Activity	Distance	Reps	Time	Rest

Difficulty: Rating:

TRAINING LOG

Date: _____ Time: _____

Warm Up

Swim Activity	Distance	Reps	Time	Rest

Sets

Swim Activity	Distance	Reps	Time	Rest

Cool Down

Swim Activity	Distance	Reps	Time	Rest

Difficulty: 🏊 🏊 🏊   Rating: ★ ★ ★ ★ ★

TRAINING LOG

Date: _____ Time: _____

Warm Up

Swim Activity	Distance	Reps	Time	Rest

Sets

Swim Activity	Distance	Reps	Time	Rest

Cool Down

Swim Activity	Distance	Reps	Time	Rest

Difficulty: 　　　　　Rating:

TRAINING LOG

Date: _____ Time: _____

Warm Up

Swim Activity	Distance	Reps	Time	Rest

Sets

Swim Activity	Distance	Reps	Time	Rest

Cool Down

Swim Activity	Distance	Reps	Time	Rest

Difficulty: 🏊 🏊 🏊   Rating: ★ ★ ★ ★ ★

TRAINING LOG

Date: _____ Time: _____

Warm Up

Swim Activity	Distance	Reps	Time	Rest

Sets

Swim Activity	Distance	Reps	Time	Rest

Cool Down

Swim Activity	Distance	Reps	Time	Rest

Difficulty: Rating:

— PERSONAL RECORDS —

Date	Swim Style	Distance	Time

PERSONAL RECORDS

Date	Swim Style	Distance	Time

— PERSONAL RECORDS —

Date	Swim Style	Distance	Time

PERSONAL RECORDS

Date	Swim Style	Distance	Time

── PERSONAL RECORDS ──

Date	Swim Style	Distance	Time

PERSONAL RECORDS

Date	Swim Style	Distance	Time

PERSONAL RECORDS

Date	Swim Style	Distance	Time

── PERSONAL RECORDS ──

Date	Swim Style	Distance	Time

PERSONAL RECORDS

Date	Swim Style	Distance	Time

PERSONAL RECORDS

Date	Swim Style	Distance	Time

PERSONAL RECORDS

Date	Swim Style	Distance	Time

PERSONAL RECORDS

Date	Swim Style	Distance	Time

PERSONAL RECORDS

Date	Swim Style	Distance	Time

PERSONAL RECORDS

Date	Swim Style	Distance	Time

PERSONAL RECORDS

Date	Swim Style	Distance	Time

— PERSONAL RECORDS —

Date	Swim Style	Distance	Time

NOTES

NOTES

NOTES

NOTES

NOTES

NOTES

NOTES

NOTES

NOTES

NOTES

NOTES

NOTES

NOTES

NOTES

NOTES

NOTES

NOTES

NOTES

NOTES

NOTES

Printed in Great Britain
by Amazon